C000155916

How to Survive Being a
DOG OWNER

CLIVE WHICHELOW *and* **MIKE HASKINS**

summersdale

HOW TO SURVIVE BEING A DOG OWNER

Summersdale Publishers Ltd
46 West Street
Chichester
West Sussex
PO19 1RP
UK

www.summersdale.com

Printed and bound in China

ISBN: 978-1-78685-263-2

Substantial discounts on bulk quantities of Summersdale books are available to corporations, professional associations and other organisations. For details contact general enquiries: telephone: +44 (0) 1243 771107 or email: enquiries@summersdale.com.

To.....................................

From................................

Introduction

So, you've got yourself a dog! An adorable pup! Man's best friend! What could possibly go wrong?

Well, unless you're very lucky, your pet pooch will have arrived completely untrained. Or, to put it another way, completely untamed. If that's the case you will now be sharing your home with a marauding beast that has an insatiable appetite, endless energy and no idea about social niceties (particularly regarding when, in polite society, it's considered acceptable to jump up to lick people's faces).

Your dog may believe they are expected to bark loudly and incessantly whenever anyone moves within 200 yards of your front door, and that they must greet visitors by thoroughly sniffing and examining their backsides (before, of course, proceeding to lick their faces).

You and your dog therefore face a period of intense training (although which of you will manage to train the other first remains to be seen). Hopefully you can look forward to years of friendship and fun together – all you have to do is assert your mastery and overcome every single one of your dog's instincts and inclinations.

What you need is an extensive volume answering all possible questions on dog-related problems and training. Well, we're not going to lie – this is not that book! But what this little volume provides instead is something that is much more valuable: it will not only help you survive being a dog owner but enable you to do so with a smile. And that is the dog's honest truth!

GOOD AND BAD THINGS ABOUT BEING A DOG OWNER

GOOD	BAD
You are living with a being that will forgive you all your bad habits	Unfortunately, some of his bad habits are even worse than yours
They love you unconditionally	Well, apart from the conditions that you feed them, take them for walks in all weathers and pick up their poo
They will be your closest friend	They will be so close that they will sit panting their stinky breath straight into your face
They will eat up your leftovers	If you don't watch where you leave your dinner you may have to make do with their leftovers

TYPES OF DOG OWNER YOU COULD BE

The no-nonsense disciplinarian who the dog humours for a while before doing whatever it likes

. . . .

A shepherd-like figure who exercises perfect control over their dog by a series of variously pitched whistles and strategic use of the phrase 'come-bye!'

. . . .

A timid, uncertain creature who has relinquished all control and decision-making to their canine companion

The owner with all the treats (who will be followed home from the park not only by their own dog but by every other dog in the vicinity)

TYPES OF DOG YOUR DOG COULD BE

The sort that would run for help if you collapsed in the street rather than finding something more exciting to do

. . . .

The sort that would inspire awe and wonder in other dog owners (for the right reasons)

. . . .

An adorable little thing that spends her life wondering why people are always cooing over her when she knows that she's really a wolf

A MAD WHIRLING DERVISH THAT DASHES AROUND YOUR HOUSE POSSESSED OF AN APPARENTLY ENDLESS SOURCE OF ENERGY

A BREAKDOWN OF HOW YOU WILL SPEND YOUR TIME AS A DOG OWNER

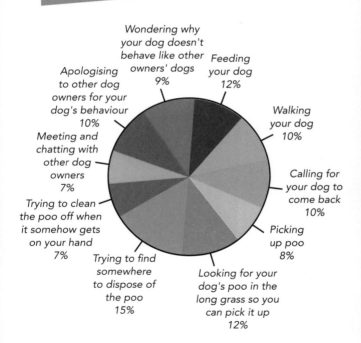

Wondering why your dog doesn't behave like other owners' dogs 9%

Feeding your dog 12%

Apologising to other dog owners for your dog's behaviour 10%

Walking your dog 10%

Meeting and chatting with other dog owners 7%

Calling for your dog to come back 10%

Trying to clean the poo off when it somehow gets on your hand 7%

Picking up poo 8%

Trying to find somewhere to dispose of the poo 15%

Looking for your dog's poo in the long grass so you can pick it up 12%

NAMES YOU SHOULDN'T CALL YOUR DOG

Anything more than two syllables long – you'll shout yourself hoarse calling them in the park

. . . .

Overly tough-sounding names like Tyson, Killer or Vlad the Impaler – these will seem particularly ridiculous if you have a chihuahua

. . . .

Very middle-class names like Quentin, Algernon or Little Lord Fauntleroy – these may provoke unwanted comments from uncouth passers-by

REALISTIC AND UNREALISTIC GOALS FOR YOUR DOG

REALISTIC	UNREALISTIC
Your dog will become one of the family	Your dog will get a job and start earning its own keep
Your dog will learn to come back when called	Your dog will learn to operate a mobile phone and come back when called long distance
You will teach your dog to fetch your newspaper	You will teach your dog to read you the newspaper
You will teach your dog to perform a dancing routine	Your dog will become an all-round family entertainer, win *Britain's Got Talent* and get their own summer season at Great Yarmouth

You will find yourself talking to strangers far more – and not just to apologise to them

. . . .

You will try one of his biscuits and get hooked on them

. . . .

To thank anyone who does anything for you you will pop a choc drop in their mouth

YOU WILL ENJOY AT
LEAST TWO GOOD
WALKS A DAY —
ONE WITH THE DOG
AND ONE TO CALM
YOURSELF DOWN
AGAIN AFTERWARDS

WAYS A DOG WILL CHANGE THE APPEARANCE OF YOUR HOUSE

What appears to be a Jackson Pollock painting on your living-room wall is actually caused by the dog shaking itself after a muddy walk

You'll often find strange slobbery patches on furniture

. . . .

Dog beds will appear in every room and trip you up – luckily, they will provide a soft landing

. . . .

What looks like a modern-art installation arrives in your hall (which is actually a pile of chewed-up tennis balls)

WAYS IN WHICH YOUR DOG WILL CHANGE YOU

You will get more exercise than ever before (whether you like it or not)

• • • • • • • • • •

Now you see what's possible, you will start trying to train your other half as well

• • • • • • • • • •

You won't think twice about picking up dog poo and may sometimes even forget to use a bag

You will regard yourself
as the leader of the
pack, and will pick up
anyone who disagrees
by the scruff of the
neck and shake them

A GUIDE TO THE ITEMS THAT A DOG OWNER WILL END UP WITH IN THEIR HOME

A dog-shaped area of the carpet with much thicker pile than the rest of it (which, on closer inspection, is actually dog hair)

. . . .

A large box containing hundreds of rolls of dog-poo bags

. . . .

A lawn that looks like a newly ploughed field following your dog's attempt at gardening

DOG TOYS
SCATTERED AT
RANDOM WHICH
MAKE A SQUEAKING
NOISE WHEN
ACCIDENTALLY
TRODDEN ON

Several half-eaten dog chews that appear in the most unlikely places

DOs AND DON'Ts AROUND THE HOUSE FOR DOG OWNERS

DO	DON'T
Allow the dog his own special place in the living room	Let him have the entire sofa
Vary her diet from time to time	Take her shopping to let her choose her own food
Give your dog the occasional scrap of chicken from your dinner	Put their bowl on the table and let them sit with you
Let your dog out into the garden when he needs to go	Let him do it in the guest bedroom if it's raining outside

Strangers nervously asking: 'Is he/
she friendly?' – they don't do that with
your spouse do they? (Do they?)

. . . .

Having to trudge around in all weathers
because the dog fancies a walk – so
that's why people buy hamsters!

Your dog panting into your face –
eventually you have to give in and stroke
them to make them turn the other way

. . . .

The regular appearance of unusual
scents around your house – if you were
choosing a fragrance dispenser, none of
these would be the smells you'd select

HOW DOGS COMMUNICATE WITH OTHER DOGS

Barking – which can mean anything from
'Good to see you' to 'I'm going to kill you'
(how they work it out is anyone's guess)

· · · · · · · · · · ·

By leaving their scent – although dogs
are mystified as to why these 'scent-
posts' always have lights on top of them

· · · · · · · · · · ·

By sniffing each other's bottoms –
it is, after all, a means to find out
quite a lot about someone else

HOW TO UNDERSTAND WHAT YOUR DOG IS TRYING TO TELL YOU

Cocking their head and listening intently – either they have heard a burglar in your house or a tin of dog food being opened

. . . .

Suddenly getting 'spooked' – either your house is haunted or your dog has just woken up from a bad dream that you are their owner

. . . .

Standing anxiously at the door – either your dog needs a wee or they've decided they've had enough of you and want to leave home

BARKING INCESSANTLY AT THE FRONT DOOR — SOMEONE IS APPROACHING THE DOOR (OR POSSIBLY ANOTHER DOOR WITHIN A HALF-MILE RADIUS)

LIKELY AND LESS LIKELY THINGS YOU MAY TEACH YOUR DOG TO DO

LIKELY	LESS LIKELY
Fetch a stick	Fetch a takeaway
Play dead	To actually do it when you're trying to impress someone with your amazing powers of command
Shake hands	Use his paws to communicate using sign language
Walk backwards	Walk backwards while making a barking noise that sounds a bit like 'Warning! Vehicle reversing!'

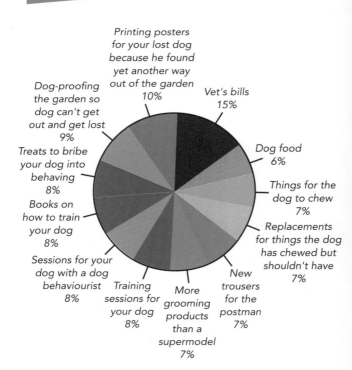

YOUR FINANCIAL OUTGOINGS FROM NOW ON

Printing posters for your lost dog because he found yet another way out of the garden
10%

Vet's bills
15%

Dog-proofing the garden so dog can't get out and get lost
9%

Dog food
6%

Treats to bribe your dog into behaving
8%

Things for the dog to chew
7%

Books on how to train your dog
8%

Replacements for things the dog has chewed but shouldn't have
7%

Sessions for your dog with a dog behaviourist
8%

Training sessions for your dog
8%

More grooming products than a supermodel
7%

New trousers for the postman
7%

THE WORST THINGS YOUR DOG WILL DO AND HOW TO LOOK AT THEM POSITIVELY

They chew a hole in your brand-new carpet – thankfully the hole is smaller than the dog basket which will now go on top of it

. . . .

They growl menacingly at an innocent passer-by – fortunately they aren't the owner of a dog that is bigger and more ferocious than yours

. . . .

They emit regular noxious odours – luckily your dog can be blamed not only for these but for any other odd smells that may arise…

It enthusiastically licks its genitals in front of polite company – it's the perfect opportunity to turn the conversation to the suppleness that can be achieved through regular exercise and yoga

HOW TO CONVINCE PEOPLE THAT YOUR DOG IS FRIENDLY

Explain that she's not baring her teeth – she's just smiling

. . . .

Tell them that the low growling sound your dog is making is the opening note of his favourite song which he wants everyone to sing along with

. . . .

Tell them that knocking them down, pinning them to the ground and sitting on top of them is just her way of saying 'hello'

DOG BEHAVIOUR THAT NON-DOG OWNERS MIGHT FIND WORRYING

Frantically digging a hole in the ground – don't worry, it's not planning to kill you and bury your body (well, probably not)

. . . .

Eating other dogs' poo – normally such commitment to recycling would be deemed admirable

. . . .

Licking their own bottom and genitals – obviously this seems totally disgusting but many owners seem to stand watching the spectacle in fascination

Eating grass – don't panic, the dog can simply be hired out to neighbours as a lawn-management service

IRRITATING THINGS OTHER DOG OWNERS WILL DO

Let their dog terrorise yours and say, 'He's only being friendly'

• • • • • • • • • •

Let their dog terrorise yours and then blame it on your dog

• • • • • • • • • •

Show off the expert control they have over their own dog

FEED YOUR DOG A MASS OF TREATS SO SHE FOLLOWS THEM BACK TO THEIR CAR AND RUNS UP THE ROAD AFTER THEM

APPROPRIATE AND INAPPROPRIATE TOYS FOR DOGS

APPROPRIATE	INAPPROPRIATE
A rubber bone	A rubber effigy of your boss
A squeaky hedgehog	A real hedgehog that is squeaking because it is terrified
A frisbee	A microlight specially made for your dog so he can fly across the park himself
A slingshot big enough to launch a ball hundreds of yards away for the dog to chase	A slingshot big enough to launch your cat hundreds of yards away for the dog to chase

APPROPRIATE AND INAPPROPRIATE TREATS FOR DOGS

APPROPRIATE	INAPPROPRIATE
Choc drops	Easter eggs and chocolate Santas
Bone-shaped biscuits	Biscuits dunked in tea
A nice big juicy bone to chew	A nice big juicy postman's leg to chew
A piece of rawhide	Your partner's favourite shoes

FAMOUS DOGS AND WHY YOURS ISN'T LIKE THEM

Scooby Doo – your dog makes a lot of strange noises but none of them could be regarded as talking

· · · · · · · · · ·

Lassie – she's been in films and TV for over 70 years, which in human years is nearly 500!

· · · · · · · · · ·

Deputy Dawg – your dog only lays down the law in your house

Goofy and Pluto – Unlike Goofy (who was a dog but acted like a person) and Pluto (who was a dog and acted like a dog), your dog doesn't think of itself as a dog at all

THINGS NON-DOG OWNERS DON'T UNDERSTAND ABOUT DOGS

People don't own dogs,
dogs own people

. . . .

Dogs are actually better company
than a lot of humans

. . . .

Running around waving your arms in
terror is unlikely to calm any dog down

*Leaning right into
a dog's face making
stupid barking noises
is not a good idea*

THE UPSIDES AND DOWNSIDES OF OWNING A DOG

UPSIDE	DOWNSIDE
They show their affection by excitedly licking you	You get to taste exactly what their dog food is like
They frighten away burglars	They also frighten away your friends, family, postmen, delivery men and everyone else
They get you out into the fresh air	You may end up out in the fresh air putting up posters asking if anyone has seen your dog
You will meet lots of other dog owners	Your dog will only let you stop and talk to owners who it knows are armed with treats

SIGNS YOU MAY BE SPOILING YOUR DOG

You occasionally treat her to a nice
juicy steak – at a posh restaurant

. . . .

You spend more money at the dog
groomers than you spend at the hairdressers

. . . .

When you throw her ball she
sits and watches you until you
go and get it back for her

He not only has a comfy bed, he also has his own comfy bedroom

BREAKDOWN OF TIME SPENT DURING A VET'S APPOINTMENT WITH YOUR DOG

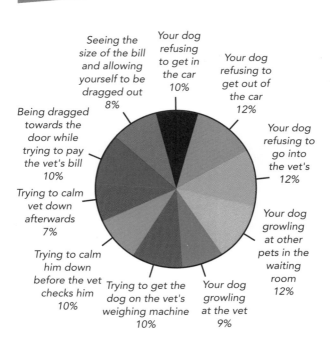

Seeing the size of the bill and allowing yourself to be dragged out 8%

Your dog refusing to get in the car 10%

Your dog refusing to get out of the car 12%

Your dog refusing to go into the vet's 12%

Being dragged towards the door while trying to pay the vet's bill 10%

Trying to calm vet down afterwards 7%

Your dog growling at other pets in the waiting room 12%

Trying to calm him down before the vet checks him 10%

Trying to get the dog on the vet's weighing machine 10%

Your dog growling at the vet 9%

WAYS IN WHICH ADVERTS FOR DOG FOOD GET IT WRONG

Hungry dogs do not usually gaze lovingly and appreciatively at their owners before being fed – they gaze accusingly at their empty bowl

. . . .

Dogs don't do heroic/adorable things to 'earn' their supper – they haul themselves out of their baskets and howl annoyingly

. . . .

Adverts don't show dogs knocking their owners over in desperation to get their food as soon as it's put out

You don't see clips of owners giving themselves hernias picking up multi-packs of food because they're on special offer

THINGS YOUR DOG WILL DO THAT WILL RESULT IN YOU NEEDING A DOCTOR'S APPOINTMENT

Suddenly chasing something while you are holding the lead, and nearly wrenching your arm out of its socket

• • • • • • • • • •

Sleeping in places that colour-match her coat so you don't see her and fall flat on your face

Take a sudden interest in sniffing something directly in your path thereby sending you flying

. . . .

Mistake you for an intruder because you went out of one door but came back in through a different one and attack you

GADGETS
A DOG OWNER MAY NEED

Your own dog-sized
X-ray machine so you
can look to see where
your car keys have got to

HIC

A poo bag made out of the same material as Harry Potter's invisibility cloak

. . . .

An air-freshener that attaches to the dog's tail

. . . .

A tracking device to find out exactly where they've been and/or how far away they are

ADVANTAGES AND DISADVANTAGES OF VERY SMALL DOGS

ADVANTAGES	DISADVANTAGES
You can simply pick them up out of any mischief they've got themselves into	If they get into a fight with a big dog they might get swallowed
They're very quick to bath	You're tempted just to run them under the tap
They don't need much exercise	You will get so fat from the lack of exercise that it can do its walk just going round you
They are incredibly cute and will be fawned over by strangers	They may be incredibly snappy when unsuspecting strangers fawn over them

ADVANTAGES AND DISADVANTAGES OF VERY LARGE DOGS

ADVANTAGES	DISADVANTAGES
Other dogs think twice about picking a fight with them	In the car they completely block out your rear view
They are very effective guard dogs	Unfortunately, all your friends are terrified of calling as well
They are loving and affectionate	If they sit on your knee, you won't be getting up again in a hurry
Their magnificent size makes quite an impression	When they go to the loo they produce something roughly the size and dimensions of a mini roundabout

SCIENTIFIC FACTS ABOUT DOGS

Dogs smell better than humans – er,
perhaps that should be: their sense
of smell is better than a human's

. . . .

Dogs have been domesticated for at
least 15,000 years – and some of them
still haven't been trained properly

. . . .

Dogs like to poo in alignment with the
earth's magnetic field – so if you want to
avoid treading in it, always carry a compass

ADVANTAGES OF DOGS OVER PARTNERS

Partners are not (usually) eternally grateful if you throw them a choc drop

. . . .

If your partner is too frisky for your liking you can't take them to the vet's for a quick operation

. . . .

Dogs will regard a visit to the park, chasing a squirrel and leaving a poo on the bowling green as a fantastic evening out

*A treat for your partner
is eating out, whereas
a treat for your dog is
eating out of the tin*

A dogspeak translator – though you might find that his vocabulary is limited to 'I'm hungry' and 'I want to go out'

. . . .

A poo detector that bleeps when you are nearing a poo (either so you can pick it up or just avoid it)

. . . .

A dog family-tree builder so you can trace your dog's pedigree – or just find a nearby tree for him and his family to wee on

FANTASIES YOU MAY START HAVING

That you and your dog have an uncanny form of communication that you can write a best-selling book about

. . . .

That your dog is a unique breed that you will be able to hire out to specialist breeders and make a fortune from

. . . .

That you will go for a walk without your dog picking a fight with any other dogs or passers-by

That your dog gets a job
as a canine model in dog-
food adverts and begins
to make enough money
to keep you in luxury

THINGS YOUR DOG WILL BRING HOME AND WHAT TO DO WITH THEM

Sticks – intertwine them to build
a lovely rose arbour framework
for your garden

• • • • • • • • • •

A collection of balls belonging to
other dogs – teach him to juggle and
become an internet sensation

• • • • • • • • • •

Fleas – train them to perform in
a flea circus and enjoy a whole
new form of pet ownership

A MOULDY OLD BONE
WHICH SHE HAS
BROUGHT HOME
TO ENJOY – DO
NOTHING: UNTIL SHE
DROPS IT OUTSIDE,
SHE IS NOT ALLOWED
BACK IN THE HOUSE

DOs AND DON'Ts WHEN TRAINING YOUR DOG

DO	DON'T
Keep commands simple	Give them in Morse code
Praise your dog when he has done well	Praise him for not biting you today
Repeat your commands until your dog responds as wanted	Repeat a series of four-letter words because your dog won't respond as wanted
Give your dog a treat when she obeys your command	Eat her treats yourself to teach her a lesson

HOW PEOPLE WILL BE ABLE TO TELL YOU ARE A DOG OWNER

You use monosyllabic commands such as 'sit', 'stay' and 'fetch' when addressing friends, family, work colleagues or shop assistants

You have one arm longer than the other due to the dog's constant tugging at the lead

. . . .

You have a very clean face because it is frequently being licked

. . . .

You have a ready supply of treats and poo bags stuffed into your pockets or handbag

ADVICE YOU WILL RECEIVE FROM OTHER DOG OWNERS AND CAN SAFELY IGNORE

'They never bite the hand that feeds them'

. . . .

'Don't worry, they always know their own way home'

. . . .

'Dogs are very conscious of their own health and will never knowingly over-eat'

. . . .

'The best way to show who is master is to take a bone out of his mouth while he's gnawing on it'

BAD REASONS FOR TAKING YOUR DOG TO THE VET

Because he smells funny

. . . .

Because she refuses point-
blank to perform tricks

. . . .

Because her wee is turning
your lawn brown

. . . .

Because you have decided to breed
from him after all and want his
neutering operation reversed

WORRIES THAT ONLY A DOG OWNER HAS TO DEAL WITH

That someone has rung your doorbell
and you have to leave your dinner
unattended for two minutes

. . . .

How well-behaved others dogs are

. . . .

Realising someone is having a picnic near
where you have just let your dog off its lead

That one day you'll
hear your mobile
phone ringing and it's
coming from somewhere
inside your dog

THINGS ONLY A DOG OWNER WOULD FIND EXCITING

Managing to balance a small hat and pair of sunglasses on your dog's head

A new flavour of dog treat

. . . .

That a well-known celebrity has
got the same breed as you

. . . .

Your dog going to sleep
in a funny position

THE IDEAL DOG vs YOUR DOG

IDEAL DOG	YOUR DOG
Doesn't bark or growl at strangers	Even barks and growls at you
Comes back when you call him in the park	Seems to completely forget who you are and disappears over the horizon at the earliest opportunity
Will let you know when an intruder has broken into your property	Will let you know when an intruder has broken into your property by hiding behind you and trembling
Exudes energy and excitement when you take her to the park	Exudes energy and excitement when you are trying to watch your favourite TV programme

SELF-HELP BOOKS YOU MIGHT WANT TO READ

How To Stop Your Dog Getting the Upper Paw in Your Relationship

• • • • • • • • • •

How to Convince People That Despite Everything It Is Actually Really Very Friendly

• • • • • • • • • •

The Dog Whisperer, The Dog Caller, The Dog Shouter and The Dog Yeller-At-The-Top-Of-His-Voice

THINGS TO KEEP TELLING YOURSELF

The reason he behaves like an animal is because he is one

. . . .

She doesn't actually speak English so she probably won't understand anything more complicated than 'sit', 'stay', 'din dins' or 'walkies!'

. . . .

All your dog really wants to do is to please you – even though this is hard to believe sometimes!

If you're interested in finding out more about our books, find us on Facebook at **Summersdale Publishers** and follow us on Twitter at **@Summersdale**.

www.summersdale.com